I0104103

Wildlife in Central America 2;

25 More Amazing Animals
Living in Tropical Rainforest and River Habitats

Text and Photography by Cyril Brass

Thank you for purchasing this book and in doing so

Receive a FREE ebook copy of the classic wildlife adventure:

"The Jungle Book"

Go to

www.wildlifearoundtheworld.com

Please visit our website at www.wildlifearoundtheworld.com for more detailed wildlife information and stunning photo image books.

Front cover image: Red-Backed Squirrel Monkey
Back cover images: Hoffmann's 2-Toed Sloth and Masked Tree Frog

Wildlife in Central America 2;

25 More Amazing Animals
Living in Tropical Rainforest and
River Habitats

Text and Photography by Cyril Brass

Table of Contents

Introduction

Welcome to Wildlife in Central America 2; 25 More Amazing Animals living in Tropical Rainforest and River Habitats part of the Wildlife Around The World Series.

This second book introduces more amazing wildlife living in Central America. With easy-to-read text and eye-catching images, curious readers will identify and learn about 25 More wildlife species living in the rainforests and rivers of Central America.

The number of wildlife species living in Central America is so extensive that we cannot provide images and information on all of them in one or two books. Included within this book is a representation of the thousands and thousands of amazing animals that live in and around the tropical rainforests and rivers of Central America.

Stunning colorful photos and descriptive text fills every engaging page providing an exciting look at the wide variety of fascinating and unusual creatures; from endangered great green macaws resting high in the treetops to collared peccary foraging on the forest ground; from skittish black river turtles swimming in the rivers and streams to colorful blue-crowned motmots sitting on branches of trees.

These informative pages provide facts and images about each of the 25 animals included in this book; what they look like, what habitat they live in, what they eat, how the parents take care of their young, how they defend themselves in the wild, and many more interesting details.

More and more readers will understand and appreciate the precious world around us by exploring and learning about the many amazing wild creatures living in different regions of the world. This book will appeal to wildlife enthusiasts and animal lovers of all ages.

About Central America

Central America is the southern geographical region in the continent of North America.

Seven countries that make up Central America: Belize, Guatemala, El Salvador, Honduras, Nicaragua, Costa Rica and Panama.

The size of Central America is 523,780 square kilometers (202,230 square miles) which is 0.1% of the Earth's surface.

The Central America land formation connects Mexico in North America to Columbia in South America.

There are bodies of water on both sides of Central America; the Pacific Ocean is on the west side and the Caribbean Sea is on the east side.

Central America is one of the most bio-diverse regions on the planet providing a wide variety of natural habitats and ecosystems. The area provides homes and food for an abundant number of wildlife species in this small geographical region.

Central America

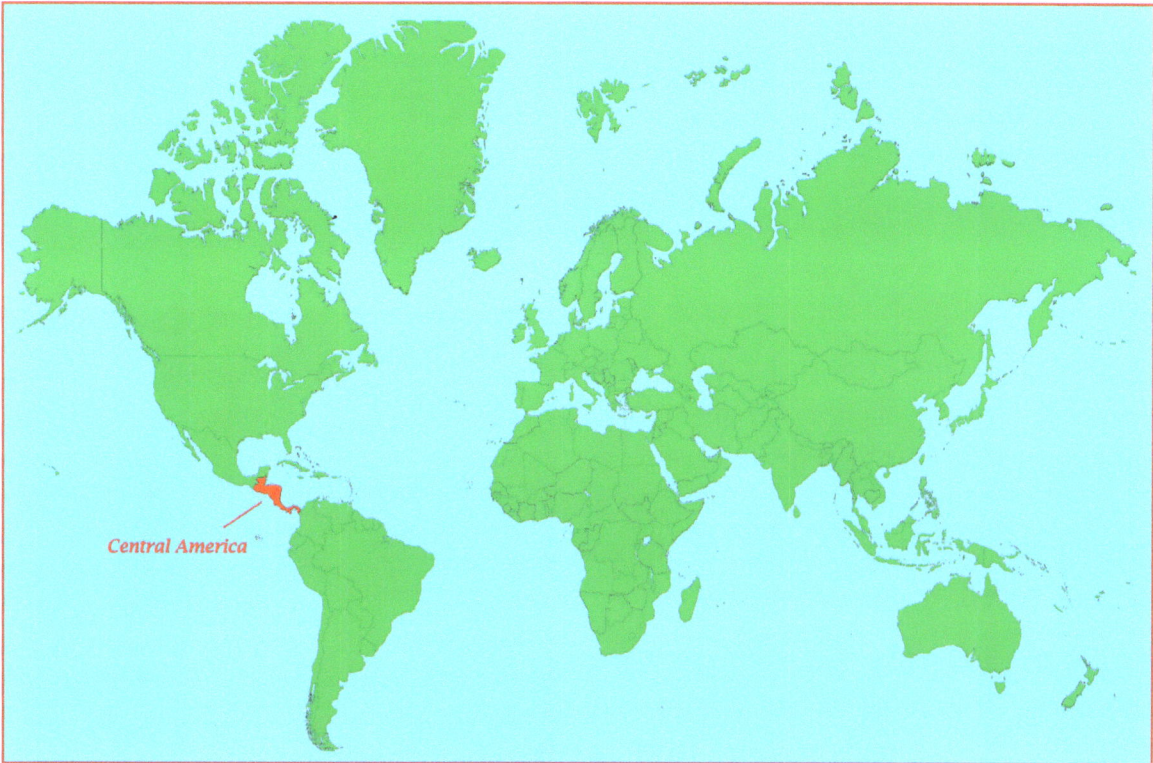
Central America

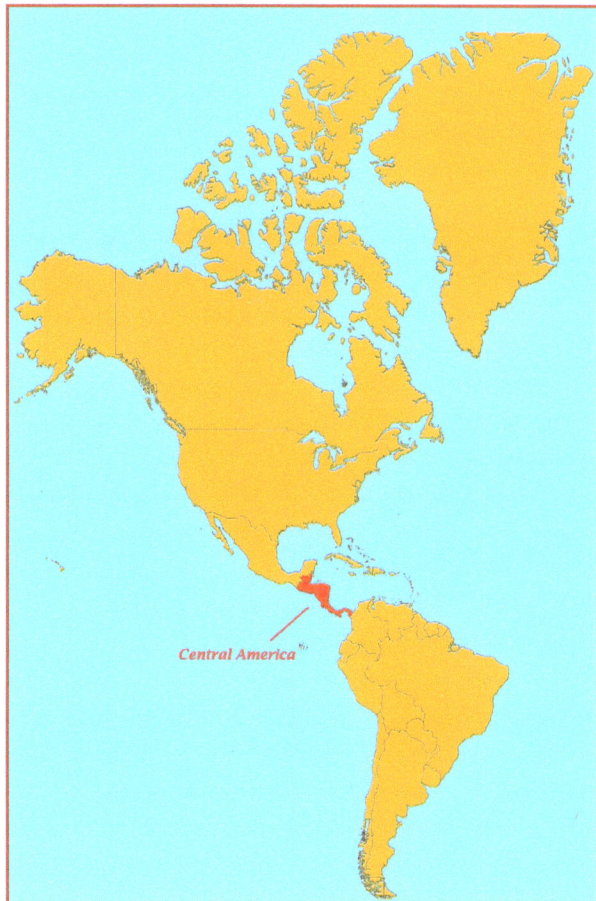
Central America

Red-Backed Squirrel Monkey
(Saimiri Oerstedii)

The Red-Backed Squirrel Monkey also called the Central American Squirrel Monkey is the smallest and rarest monkey in Central America. This colorful primate is a very social intelligent creature living in large groups called "troops".

It is an arboreal diurnal creature spending almost all of its life in the trees, watching everything that is happening around him in the trees or below on the ground. This monkey species in the only Central American monkey without a prehensile tale. The long tail provides balance when it travels through the treetops but not used for grasping branches for support.

This active and curious creature moves rapidly and noisily through the forest leaping from branch to branch checking every nook, branch, and leaf in search of food. Being omnivores it eats a variety of foods such as flowers, leaves, buds, nuts, insects, small lizards, and eggs.

The Red-Backed Squirrel Monkey is highly endangered due to loss of habitat, pesticide usage, and illegal pet trade.

Collared Peccary

(Tayassu Tajacu)

The Collared Peccary has the appearance of a hog or pig but is in its own classification. Its coarse coat is a blend of black and white colors. A white collar runs around the shoulders and neck is what gives this species its name.

This smelly creature is sometimes called a "musk hog" because of the odor it emits from the glands near its eyes and on its rump. A strong musky smell remains in the air along the forest trails where the herd recently passed.

The Collared Peccary has a highly sensitive nose which allows it to find and dig out food from beneath the ground. Its presence in the rainforest is also evident by the disturbed soil where it has uprooted roots, tubers, invertebrates and small vertebrates.

This species has a close social relationship living in hierarchical herds. Having strong hearing but poor vision it relies on each other's vocalizations to communicate with each other. It lives in burrows dug under tree roots or logs as well as in caves.

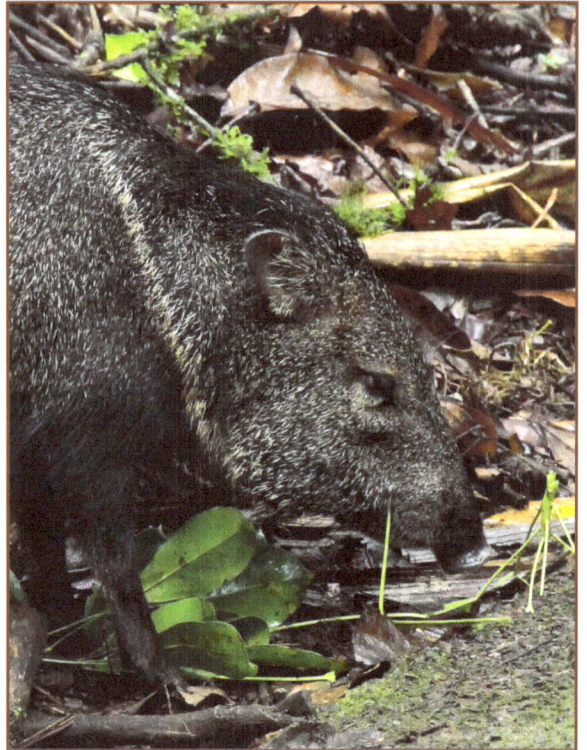

The Collared Peccary is considered a seed destroyer instead of a seed disperser. This animal chews the seeds with its molars, destroying the seeds ability to generate new growth in the forest.

Hoffmann's Two-Toed Sloth
(Choloepus Hoffmanni)

The Hoffmann's Two-Toed Sloth is a solitary, non-territorial, arboreal animal living in lowland humid tropical forests.

The most prominent characteristic that makes the two-toed sloth different from the three-toed sloth is the number of fingers on its forelimbs. Two-toed sloth have two functioning fingers with sharp claws and three-toed sloth have three functioning clawed fingers but each species has three toes.

This sloth species is mostly a nocturnal creature. After a day of sleeping and hanging out in the trees, it begins to move in search of food throughout the darkness of the night. Primarily a herbivore, the Two-Toed Sloth eats a more varied diet of leaves, twigs, buds, and fruits but sometimes will eat small rodents and insects.

The excellent camouflage and slow movements in the trees help to conceal itself from predators such as harpy eagles, anacondas, jaguars, ocelots and humans. But if it does get spotted by an attacker, the Hoffman's Two-Toed Sloth will defend itself by biting with its large canine teeth, similar to carnivore animals or swinging its arms with its claws.

Proboscis Bat

(Rhynchonycteris Naso)

The Proboscis Bat is one of the smallest bat species in Central America growing up to 6 centimeters (2.4 inches). It is identified by its long fleshy pointed nose and by the two broken wavy white lines through the gray-brown fur along the back and the pale colored fur along the forearms.

The Proboscis Bat like all other bat species is born with the ability to fly, but at birth, its wings are too small to take flight. It is the only mammal naturally capable of flying.

Small groups of Proboscis Bats roost very close to water sources in the tropical lowlands. This nocturnal bat can be seen sleeping during the day on tree trunks, in an unusual formation, hanging upside down aligned in a straight vertical row nose to tail nose to tail.

Feeding begins as the sun begins to set. This flying insectivore travels close to the surface of the water where it swoops and dives through the air capturing insects emerging from its aquatic larvae stage of development.

It orients its self through the darkness of night using echo sounds bouncing back from its ultrasonic cries.

Northern Tamandua
(Tamandua Mexicana)

The Northern Tamandua, also known as the Collared Anteater, Banded Anteater or Lesser Anteater, is under the classification with sloths and armadillos. The name Tamandua comes from the Tupi Indian words; "Taa" meaning ant and "Mandeu" meaning trap – anttrap.

Anteaters have absolutely no teeth. The specially adapted mouth can only open a small amount just enough to stick out its long tongue that has tiny sticky barbs designed to capture the miniature prey. The tongue can measure up to 40 centimeters (15.75 inches).

A solitary nocturnal animal, the Northern Tamandua has a black shaped vest over the gold or tan fur which blends into the surroundings. While traveling in the forest, it easily navigates branches using its enormous hand claws and a prehensile tail. It is mostly an arboreal animal but can be seen foraging for food on the ground.

It searches for tasty insects in nests high up in trees, in fallen logs and in termite mounds on the ground. The anteater rips open the hideouts exposing colonies of endless amounts of scurrying ants or termites, which are quickly lapped up with its sticky tongue.

Green and Black Poison Dart Frog

(Dendrobates Auratus)

The Green and Black Poison Dart Frog is the largest poison dart arrow frog species growing up to 4.0 centimeters (1.58 inches). This non-territorial semi-arboreal amphibian is most active in early morning and late afternoon foraging among leaf litter on the forest floor, fallen logs as well as in trees and shrubs.

With its random pattern of green and black patches, this bright coloration sends a warning signal to any predator to stay away, for it possesses poisonous glands on the skin that will emit toxic secretions, potentially paralyzing or killing the attacker. The toxic substance comes from the food it eats, in particular, the many ants it consumes each day.

Even though this frog lives near streams or pools of waters in tropical lowland habitats, it is a poor swimmer due to having no webbing between its toes. Instead with the sticky pads at the end of its toes provide suction for the frog to climb on rocks and up tree trunks.

The Green and Black Poison Dart Frogs are excellent parents. After a female lays her 6 or so eggs in a shallow pool of water, her mate frequently checks on the eggs keeping them moist during the two weeks it takes for them to hatch.

One by one, each tadpole climbs onto its father's back and is carried to a bigger source of water, where it continues the transformation into adult frogs.

Masked Tree Frog

(Smilisca Phaeota)

The Masked Tree Frog is identified by the black markings that appear from the tip of nose continuing through the eyes and eardrum along its face. This black Zorro-type mask enhances the frog's camouflage by hiding the shape of the eyes, which is what predators will use to detect its prey.

The nocturnal Mask Tree Frog lives in humid lowland forest habitats in the tropics. This non-venomous amphibian must rely on its camouflage within the trees and vegetation to protect itself from predators. It has the ability to change its color ranging from light tan to olive green adapting to its current surroundings.

This frog is well adapted for life in the trees with its long legs and large sticky toe pads. With excellent jumping ability, the Masked Tree Frog is able to quickly escape potential dangers that approach.

The female Masked Tree Frog can lay up to 2,000 eggs in one clutch which is deposited into a nearby source of water. The eggs float in the water until they hatch within one day. The tadpoles stay in the same body of water until their final metamorphosis is completed.

Giant Toad
(Bufo Marinus)

The Giant Toad is also known as the Cane Toad, Giant Neotropical Toad or Marine Toad. This nocturnal terrestrial toad is difficult to confuse with other toads mostly because of its massive size. During the day, it is found hiding under the cover of rocks and logs and comes out at night to eat.

Another distinctive trait is the pair of large, triangularly shaped poison glands on the sides of the neck. The glands in an adult contain enough toxins to kill large animals. The Giant Toad also has bony ridges above the eyes along the top of its head and scattered warts all over its skin.

Its body color is brown, gray to olive green, with brown splotches on a dirty white or cream underside.

The Giant Toad is non-territorial covering an enormous range as it is easily adaptable to a variety of habitats. It does not rely on one or two food sources. With such a diverse diet and enormous appetite, this predator will eat almost anything including insects, spiders, stinging wasps, toxic millipedes, and other small vertebrates such as mice, lizards, and other frog species. It will even consume fruit and plant matter if need be.

Golfodulcean Poison Dart Frog
(Phyllobates Vittatus)

The Golfodulcean Poison Dart Frog is a brightly colored black-dark brown frog with a pair of wide orange stripes down the top of the head and along the smooth sloping back. The limbs are a turquoise color dotted with black spots. The sides of the body are a blue or green marbled pattern.

It has highly potent toxins in its skin. The toxicity is advertised by its multi-colored body to any predator. These toxins are believed to come from particular insects it eats. The insects acquire the poison from the plants they consume.

This terrestrial amphibian is most active at dawn and dusk but is rarely seen as it stays close to its hiding places near fallen logs, rock crevices or low dense vegetation in shaded areas of the forest floor. It moves by walking interspersed with rapid hops.

The Golfodulcean Poison Dart Frog is endemic to Costa Rica, inhabiting the wet forests and lowlands of the southwestern region of Costa Rica. It is listed as an endangered species due to the decline of its habitat and water contamination.

American Crocodile
(Cebus Capucinus)

The American Crocodile, which is related to caimans and alligators, ranges in colors from brownish gray, dark olive to grayish green with dark colored bands across the back and tail.

It can be seen basking in the sun lying motionless on sand bars, shorelines and river banks. This cold-blooded reptile requires the heat from the sun to warm its body. But when the body temperature increases too high, it will submerge its body underwater or if it stays on land will open its huge mouth to cool down.

This prehistoric looking carnivore must tip its head upwards in order to swallow its prey as it is unable to swallow with its head in a horizontal position. It feeds on a variety of aquatic animals; crabs, frogs, fish, waterfowl and small to medium mammals coming too close to the water's edge.

The American Crocodile lives in salt, brackish or freshwater habitats in or near swamps, mangrove estuaries, lagoons, wetlands, and rivers. This massive reptile is an excellent swimmer using its powerful tail to propel itself through the water. It is able to remain submerged underwater for more than an hour.

REPTILES

Brown Basilisk

(Basiliscus Basiliscus)

The Brown Basilisk is known for its ability to run across the water upright on its hind legs, thus the common name of Jesus Christ Lizard. This ability to quickly run on the surface of the water is from its large web-like hind feet with extensive long toes covering a large area of water. Other names are Striped Basilisk and Common Basilisk.

This lizard is mostly brown with light and dark stripes on the body; dark stripes on the flanks and dorsal crest and lighter stripes extending from eyes to hind legs. It has a triangular crest on the head with a smaller ridge along the back and tail.

The brown coloration with unique markings provides excellent camouflage while resting on low hanging branches or on fallen trees on the ground. This basilisk will remain motionless for long periods and therefore is difficult to detect.

Being both an arboreal and terrestrial reptile, it can quickly move on the forest floor and easily climb on vegetation and branches. This omnivorous lizard is active during the day, searching for leaves, flowers, and fruit or hunting for invertebrates or small vertebrates. At night the Brown Basilisk sleeps on leaves and branches close to water so when threatened or attacked, allows for a quick escape.

Ctenosaur

(Ctenosaura Similis)

The Ctenosaur, also called the Black Iguana or Spiny Tailed Iguana, is a close relative to the Green Iguana. This is a highly adaptable reptile capable of living in a variety of habitats with the primary requirement of hot sunshine within the habitat.

This iguana species is darker-colored and lacks the iguana's conspicuous head spines and crest. It possesses a massive head with small dewlap and dorsal crest. The robust body has dark bands near the back section of the body, muscular limbs, and razor sharp claws. The long thick tail is covered with small sharp spines.

The male performs a head bobbing motion as a warning sign to approaching intruders to stay away. This action is also used to attract potential females.

This semi-arboreal lizard spends most of the day foraging for food or basking in the sun. It can be seen stretched out high in the treetops, clinging onto branches of lower vegetation, resting motionless on fallen trees and large rocks or walking along forest trails and on sandy beaches.

The Ctenosaur is predominantly a herbivore eating leaves, flowers, and fallen fruits but is also an opportunistic creature eating insects, spiders, crabs, small lizards and small birds.

Black River Turtle

(Rhinoclemmys Funerea)

The Black River Turtle is a semi-aquatic terrestrial turtle living in humid tropical forests close to freshwater swamps, marshes, ponds or slow flowing rivers. It is also known as the Black Wood Turtle.

The carapace of this turtle is a smooth shell with a high dome shape. The limbs are covered with speckled yellow markings on its legs, neck, and head. The extensive webbing on its toes and fingers enables it to be an efficient swimmer.

Much of the day is spent basking on partially submerged logs, sandbars or thick vegetation close to the water's edge. This skittish reptile is easily frightened by any sense of danger approaching. It quickly dives into the water where it can remain submerged for several minutes before surfacing in a different location.

The Black River Turtle ventures onto land at night to forage for grass, leaves, and fruit to eat. As well, the female lays up to four eggs on the ground covered with leaves and other plant materials.

Delicate Whiptail

(Ameiva Leptophrys)

The Delicate Whiptail, also called the Delicate Ameiva, is identified by the dark brown zig-zag lines running down each side of the body and by the long whip-like tail which is usually twice as long as the body.

This terrestrial ground dwelling lizard is mostly brown or copper-brown in color with a bluish-white belly and narrow pointed head.

This highly alert and active lizard moves throughout the fallen leaves and plant materials. It forages for food along the ground poking its nose in the leaf litter and under sticks and rocks. Its diet is primarily insects and other small arthropods.

The Delicate Whiptail can also be seen foraging on a beach for tiny amphipod crustaceans and salty marine creatures. It possesses a nasal salt gland to excrete the excess salt it has ingested.

This tropical reptile lives in open sunny habitats and can be frequently seen along forest trails, on the side of roads and close to sandy beaches. Its day is spent exploring on the ground for food or sitting motionless sunning themselves on rocks or fallen logs.

Great Green Macaw

(Ara Ambigua)

The Great Green Macaw is a large brilliantly colored parrot with intense green plumage on the body, on the head with a puffy red brow, on the wings with blue wingtips, and red tail feathers. The large black beak is well adapted for cracking open very hard nuts of the almond tree.

This colorful bird is usually vocal during flight and quiet when perched on a branch or while eating. It has a steady flight movement through the air with slow shallow wingbeats. This bird species rarely gathers and hangs out in large flocks. Instead, it is usually seen in pairs with its life-long mating partner.

Inhabiting forest edges of lowland tropical rainforest, this macaw is a habitat specialist, an extremely picky parrot depending on almost entirely on a single species of tree, the wild almond tree. This tree provides most of its food resources and nesting needs.

The Great Green Macaw is a highly endangered bird. Its life and survival are critically dependent on the continued existence of the wild almond tree. Its population has also decreased through illegal hunting and pet trade. It is a valuable animal for the rainforest as it helps rebuild the forest being a seed disperser.

Blue-Crowned Motmot
(Momotus Momota)

The Blue-Crowned Motmot, which is grouped with the kingfisher and bee-eater species, is a mid-size bird with bright colorful plumage. Both male and female look the same with blue on the head, a black facial mask with blue edging, a bluish green throat, a longish down-curved bill with serrated edges, a greenish to yellowish-orange-olive belly and chest with a small dark spot and a long blue tail.

The long tennis racquet tipped tail habitually sways like a pendulum from side to side while sitting quietly on a branch in the understory of forests.

The nest of this bird species is at the end of a long burrow that is dug into an earth embankment along creeks, rivers, roadsides or steep hillsides. The burrow can be several meters (feet) deep from the entrance. The female lays up to 4 eggs in a clutch. Both parents incubate the eggs and care for its offspring.

The Blue-Crowned Motmot is a sit-and-wait predator that will sit perched on horizontal branches quietly for long periods of time, watching below for small lizards, snakes, insects, and invertebrates. After capturing its prey, the Motmot returns to a perch to eat its catch. It also eats fruits and seeds.

Great Egret
(Ardea Alba)

The Great Egret, also known as the Common Egret or Great White Heron, is the largest of the all-white heron species. Unlike other heron species who change color from a hatchling into a mature bird, the Great Egret has pure white plumage at all ages.

It has a distinctive long S-shaped neck, yellowish-orange dagger-like bill, and long black legs. These long legs enable it to hunt in the deeper waters where other water birds are unable to go.

This Egret catches its prey by wading slowly through the wetlands or standing motionless in water for long periods waiting for unsuspecting prey to come within the striking range of its long neck and razor-sharp bill. This bird is a carnivore eating mainly fish and crabs.

It lives in wetlands with freshwater, brackish and saltwater habitats near rivers, streams, swamps, lagoons, and estuaries. The Great Egret nests in trees near water sources and gather in groups called colonies, which may include other heron or egret species.

The Great Egret is a monogamous bird, with both parents incubating the three to four eggs and raising its young.

Yellow-Crowned Night Heron

(Nyctanassa Violacea)

The Yellow-Crowned Night Heron is a small to medium-sized water bird whose habitats are within the brackish water of mangrove swamps and lagoons or within freshwater lowland streams, rivers, and estuaries.

Both the male and female look alike having a black head with a large white patch on each cheek, a creamy yellow crown and head plumes, a thick short bill, orange eyes, a short neck, a purple-gray stocky body and short yellow legs.

This nocturnal heron forages at night by slowly stalking its prey or by waiting motionless at the water's edge to ambush its victims such as crustaceans, mollusks, frogs, snails, crabs, aquatic insects and small fish. It is a solo hunter with a forward leaning posture, ready to strike in a split second.

It can also be seen in the daytime searching for food when tidal water levels have receded making an ideal feeding area.

The Yellow-Crowned Night Heron often nests in small colonies along swamps and marshes. The nest is a platform of sticks in trees or shrubs that overhang the water.

Tiger Longwing Butterfly

(Heliconius Hecale)

The Tiger Longwing Butterfly has large broad forewings with rounded tips. It varies in colors and patterns of orange, yellow and black. Other names of this butterfly are Hecale Longwing, Golden Helicon, Golden Longwing, Tiger Longwing Hecale and Passionflower Butterfly.

The strikingly bright colors of this butterfly species are a warning sign to birds that it is poisonous containing toxins that will make the attackers sick if it eats this insect. The cyanide poison is manufactured by the caterpillar from devouring the passion flower leaves.

This butterfly relies on this specific plant to provide that toxic chemical for its defense against predators.

It has a delicate fluttering flight pattern especially when hovering over a flower.

Unlike other butterflies, the female Heliconius feed on pollen and nectar.

The Tiger Longwing Butterfly is very common and easily spotted in a wide range of tropical habitats. It lives for up to nine months, much longer than most butterfly species which live only a few days or weeks.

Malachite Butterfly

(Siproeta Stelenes)

The Malachite Butterfly gets its name from the bright green colored wings which resemble the color of the malachite mineral. It lives in subtropical evergreen or semi-deciduous forests.

The upper side of the wing is colored with brilliant greens or yellowish-greens and black. The wing's underside has the same black markings but is highlighted with an orange-brown and olive-green translucent coloration.

A Malachite Butterfly's mouth is a proboscis that looks and is used like a straw. It feeds mostly on the nectar from flowers or on juices of rotting fruit.

Beginning as a spiny black caterpillar with red color markings and prominent horns on its head, it is an aggressive eater quickly growing, then transforming into a lime green chrysalis covered with pink spots and finally evolving into a stunning green and black adult butterfly.

The Malachite Butterfly, like all butterflies, is cold-blooded unable to regulate its own body temperature. If it gets too cold it cannot fly or eat. That is why it is often seen basking in the sun with its wings open allowing the veins in the wings to absorb the heat and carry that warmth to the rest of the body.

INSECTS

Sundown Cicada

(Fidicina sp.)

The Sundown Cicada can be found in rainforests and dry forests. It is known for its non-stop siren-like call mostly heard in the late afternoon in the rainforests but in the dry forests can be heard throughout the day. Zzzzzzzzzzzzzzzzzzzzeeeeeeeeeeeeee!

This is a large cicada species with big bulging eyes and a pair of long transparent veiny wings. It can reach a size up to 4 centimeters (1.6 inches).

The female lays a mass of white eggs on leaves. When the eggs hatch, the nymphs drop to the ground and burrow into the ground to feed on the juices of plant and tree roots. Most of its life is spent underground. When fully grown, the nymph digs its way to the surface of the forest floor.

During the night's darkness, the Sundown Cicada emerges from its exoskeleton and takes on a new form as a winged insect.

Above ground, the Sundown Cicada lives for only a few weeks or months. During this short time period, the female and male will mate, the female lays her eggs and both soon die afterwards.

Cone-Headed Katydid

(Copiphora Rhinoceros)

The Cone-Headed Katydid, also known as the Rhinoceros Spearbearer, is a grasshopper-like insect with a distinctive cone-shaped spear extended from its forehead at the base of the antennae. It also differs from a grasshopper by having an extremely long threadlike antennae which is two to three times the length of the body. The female has a long ovipositor.

Its plant-like appearance allows it to blend into the surrounding vegetation. This mimicry of shape and color to leaves protects this katydid from potential predators. The Cone-Headed Katydid is a poor flyer but can jump quickly to escape danger.

It lives in habitats with lots of plants in Neotropical low elevation rainforests and second growth forests. This nocturnal solitary non-social creature will spend most of its life on the plants that it will consume. It feeds on leaves, stems, flowers, and fruit seeds.

Unlike most katydids who are herbivores, this omnivorous species is an active predator attacking snails and other katydid species with a powerful bite using its large jaw.

To attract females, the male Cone-Headed Katydid makes loud high pitched chirps while the body trembles that causes vibrations to the surrounding plants. The front wings have special structures that can be rubbed together to make sounds.

ARACHNIDS

Golden Orb-Weaver
(Nephila Clavipes)

The Golden Orb-Weaver is not named by the brightly colored female of yellow, green and black with yellow speckles. Instead, its name is derived by the yellow silk, which the female uses to weave her web. The bright sun rays illuminate these yellow fibers into a golden reflective orb. Other names of this arachnid are Golden Silk Orb-Weaver, Giant Wood Spider, and Banana Spider.

This skillful architect and hunter builds a complex network of silk strings, the largest and strongest webs of all arachnids. The silk used to spin its cylindrical orbs possesses incredible strength enabling the spider to construct a secure protective barricade as well as an effective trap for unsuspecting insects.

Upside down, the female positions herself in the center of her trap, patiently waiting for something tasty to land on or fly into her sticky maze. Once the captured prey becomes entangles in the web, the female bites

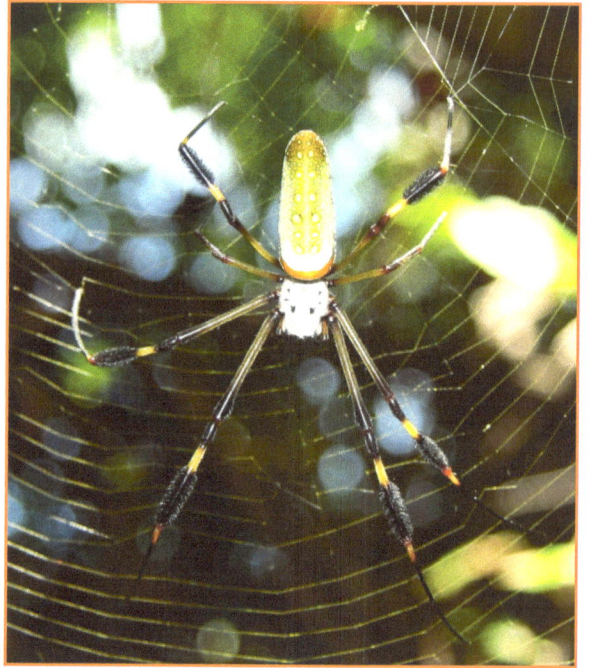

injecting deadly venom into the victim. If the victim is quite big she will wrap it with silk before eating it.

There is a huge size difference between the female and male Golden Orb-Weaver. The dull reddish brown colored male is three to four times smaller than the female. The tiny male is often unnoticed on the web to any hungry predator and sometimes even to the female.

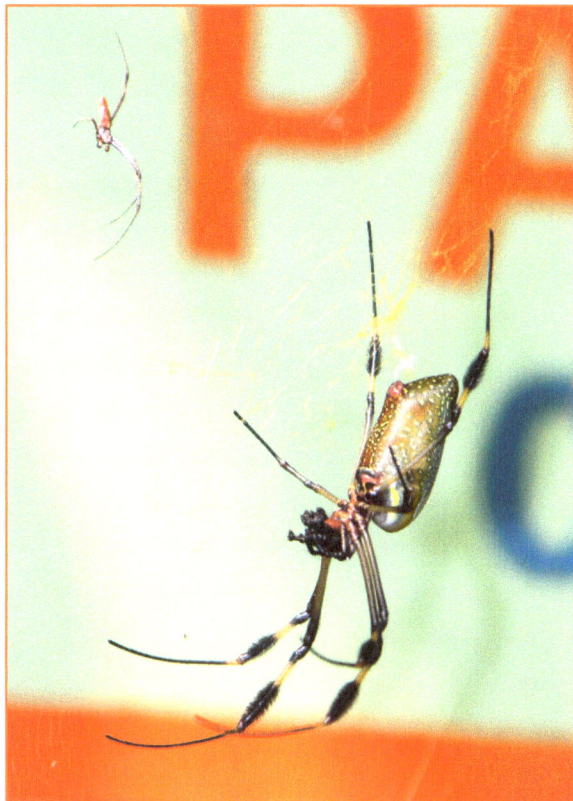

Mouthless Orange Crab

(Gecarcinus Quadratus)

The Mouthless Orange Crab is a colorful land crab with a bright orange-red body and legs, a black carapace and a pair of large purple front claws. Other names are Moon Crab, Mouthless Crab, Harlequin Land Crab, Halloween Crab, and Jack-o-Lantern Crab.

It lives in tropical habitats such as mangroves, sand dunes and lowland forests near Pacific coastal waters. This crab species travels to the coastal waters to mate and where the female lays her eggs. Possessing gills, allows this arthropod to venture into the water.

This terrestrial omnivorous crab forages mostly at night for leaf litter, seedlings and sometimes animal tissue gathered from the forest floor. It carries the food back to its burrow before consuming it.

It is primarily a nocturnal creature but can be seen during the day scurrying about on the ground, then quickly hiding into its burrow. Each crab digs its own burrow deep into the forest floor which may reach 1.50 meters (5 feet).

The Mouthless Orange Crab plays an important ecological role by carrying leaves into its burrows which contribute to nutrient cycling. By eating a variety of seeds it determines the future plant growth in that particular area of the rainforest.

Ghost Crab

(Ocypode Gaudicaudii)

The Ghost Crab gets its name from its ability to disappear from sight as it speedily retreats into its burrow under the sandy beaches of tropical and subtropical areas.

It has distinctive purple to black eyes on long vertical stalks protruding high above the body. These alien-like eyestalks allow for 360-degree vision for the crab.

The Ghost Crab is a pale gray to reddish-orange in color with sandy dots across the top of the carapace. A young crab is a mottled gray-brown with gray eyestalks blending into the sand.

This crab species lives on the sandy beaches spending its time digging up burrows after the high tidal waters recede. Hours are spent excavating its burrow dumping and tamping sand away from the entrance. The burrow is a long tunnel with a chamber at the end. Sometimes there is a second entrance to the burrow.

It is more active at night but can be seen during the day. At dusk, before dark, it scurries to the ocean to obtain oxygen from the water which it stores in sacs near the gills. During the night this omnivorous creature eats algae, dead plant and animal materials that have been washed ashore by the ocean's waves.

Glossary of Terms

Amphibian (n)	an animal that is able to live both in water and on land
Amphipod Crustacean (n)	is a type of malacostraca crustaceans with no carapace and generally with laterally compressed bodies.
Arachnid (n)	a group of small animals similar to insects but with four pairs of legs
Arboreal (adj)	the lifestyle of an animal living in trees
Arthropod (n)	an invertebrate animal that has an external skeleton, a segmented body and jointed limbs
Basking (v)	the behavior of resting in the sun as a way of raising the body temperature, commonly performed by cold-blooded animals
Bird (n)	an animal that is a feathered, winged, bipedal, warm-blooded, egg-laying, vertebrate animal
Brackish (adj)	slightly briny or salty water
Burrow (n)	a hole or tunnel dug in the ground by a small animal
Camouflage (n)	a condition in which the appearance of an animal when placed against a background makes the animal difficult or impossible to see
Carapace (n)	a bony shield or shell covering some or all of the dorsal part of an animal
Carnivore (n)	an animal that eats meat
Chrysalis (n)	the hard-shelled pupa of a moth or butterfly
Clutch (n)	the eggs that are laid in a single nest usually by a single female
Colony (n)	a group of the same kind of animals living together
Dewlap (n)	a fold of fleshy skin that hangs down from the chin and throat area
Diurnal (adj)	an animal that is active during daylight hours
Dorsal (adj)	of or on the back or upper surface of an animal
Endangered (adj)	at high risk and threatened with extinction
Endemic (adj)	belonging exclusively or confined to a particular place
Estuaries (n)	area where part of the mouth of river current meets the ocean's tide
Exoskeleton (n)	a rigid external covering for the body in some invertebrate animals, especially arthropods, providing both support and protection
Flock (n)	a group of birds
Forage (v)	to wander or go in search of something
Forewing (n)	the two front wings of a four-winged insect
Habitat (n)	an ecological or environmental area where a particular species of animal lives
Herbivore (n)	an animal that eats plant materials
Insect (n)	an animal that has an exoskeleton, a three-part body, three pairs of jointed legs, compound eyes and one pair of antennae

Insectivore (n)	an animal that eats insects
Invertebrate (n)	an animal that lacks a spinal column
Larva (n)	the immature stage of an animal prior to metamorphosis
Mammal (n)	an animal in which the female gives live birth, not eggs and feeds them on milk from her own body
Metamorphosis (n)	the process by which the creature like an insect or amphibian changes its form from an egg to a caterpillar to a cocoon to a moth or butterfly; from an egg to a nymph to an adult; or from an egg to a tadpole to a frog
Monogamous (adj)	a single female and male create a pair bond with each other and do not have multiple mates
Nocturnal (adj)	active at night
Non-Venomous (adj)	a creature that does not possess a poisonous substance used for protection against predators
Nymph (n)	an immature form of an insect
Omnivore (n)	an animal that eats a variety of food that may include plant, animals, algae, fungi and bacteria
Ovipositor (n)	a tubular organ through which a female insect or fish deposits eggs
Plumage (n)	the feathers of a bird
Predator (n)	an animal that hunts other animals for food
Prehensile tail (n)	a tail that can be curled to grip a branch and that can support part of all of the animal's weight
Prey (n)	an animal that is being attacked by another animal
Proboscis (n)	a slender tubular organ on the head of an invertebrate used for sucking or piercing
Rainforest (n)	a forest located in a hot region of the world that receives a lot of rain
Reptile (n)	an animal whose blood temperature changes according to the outside temperature and whose bodies are covered by hard material such as scales or plates
Seed destroyer (n)	an animal that eats seeds that are unable to regenerate
Seed disperser (n)	an animal that moves or transports seeds away from the parent plant
Semi-Aquatic (adj)	able to live both on land and in the water
Solitary (adj)	living alone without others
Species (n)	a group of closely related animals that possess common characteristics and freely inter-breed in nature and produce fertile offspring
Submerged (adj)	covered with water completely
Terrestrial (adj)	living on the ground
Territorial (adj)	an act by an animal by defending a habitat or region against other animals of the same species
Toxin (n)	a substance produced by a living creature that is poisonous to other creatures
Translucent (adj)	permitting light to pass through but diffusing it so opposite side is not clearly visible
Understory (n)	smaller trees, shrubs and vegetation that grow within a taller forest
Vertebrate (n)	an animal that has a spinal column
Wetland (n)	land areas where the water covers the soil or is near the surface of the soil all year such as marshes and swamps
Wildlife (n)	non-domesticated animal species living in nature

Index

About the Photographer and Author

Published author and freelance wildlife photographer Cyril Brass presents a combination of informative text and unique photographs detailing many interesting characteristics and behaviors about many wildlife species living in the Tropical Rainforest and River Habitats of Central America.

Cyril has always been interested in wild animals in far-off countries. Once he caught the travel bug he was able to learn and photograph first-hand, encountering many wildlife species he had only read about or seen on TV.

For many years, Cyril has been exploring wildlife all around the world; from sloths and toucans in the tropical rainforests of Central America to elephants and lions on the savannas of East Africa.

His wildlife book series covers informative details and colorful images of many amazing animals living in different habitats and regions around the world for readers of all ages to enjoy.

www.ingramcontent.com/pod-product-compliance
Lightning Source LLC
Chambersburg PA
CBHW060822270326
41931CB00002B/51